BELONGS TO:

Made in the USA
Monee, IL
28 May 2022

97157616R00069